RED ROCK DREAMING

Evocations of life on the Levant Coast
by Stanza Alacant

Published by McFarlands Publishing

RED ROCK DREAMING

McFarlands Publishing
11-13 Victoria Street
Douglas
Isle of Man

ISBN 978-0-9575104-2-5

Acknowledgements

Stanza Alacant
owe a special debt of gratitude to the
kind access given to the first–class facilities of the
Sede Universitaria de Benissa, C/Purissima 57-59, Benissa,
directed by Isabel Santa-Maria Perez of Alicante University
and managed by Tere Palacios Más.

The anthology was collated and edited by
Christopher North, Jane Sargeant and Rod Davis.
The Cover Picture is from a painting
by Jane Sargeant.

Introduction

Landscape informs in some magical way all that we do. For writers it is the frequent backcloth to development of imagination. A sense of place is a vital constituent in the work of a novelist and it is even more important for the poet.

The magic of landscape is powerfully at work when you first visit the Levantine coast. You notice at once the mountains, a limestone range of sudden bulk and distinctive character. Their massive scale and changing tones and colour before the intense blue of the Mediterranean is unforgettable. The Montgó Sierra for example – an almost animal presence; a great pink hog's back basking, nose towards the blue band of the sea. And then there's the crazed ridge line of the huge Sierra Bernia, the great rock of Calpe and the dreaming presence of Puigcampana.

These were the immediate impressions I had when, on a gap year trip in 1964, I was experiencing mainland Spain for the first time. I was with my brother and a close friend – driving a restored and very temperamental Bedford Dormobile. Spain was to us simply exotic – it smelt and tasted of Africa. There was dark light and searing light and villages that seemed like organisms growing out of the cut and tortured landscape. We drove over mountain passes, encountered packs of feral dogs, were holed up in a cow-shed for a while, heard some serious flamenco, made camp in an olive grove that turned out to be a trysting place for village prostitutes, got billed as the 'Los Beatles' in a village bar causing a near riot in Estartit – but the experience that stayed with me afterwards was that first sighting of the Levant coast from Denia down to Orihuela, I believe I had a premonition that one day it would be my home. It came to be: I was married in Alicante in 1967 to Maria-Luisa Lillo-Verdu, an Alicantina mixed with a dash of Cordoban Andaluz. In 2002 we came to Relleu in the Marina Baja to live.

I started writing and reading poetry as a schoolboy but in 1989 it gained serious focus after I attended a week long work-shop in Provence with the founder of the Arvon Foundation, John Fairfax. Back in England he recommended I look around for a local poetry workshop. We lived in Buckinghamshire and it seemed none were within reach – so with a friend we started our own: 'Metroland Poets'. It worked well and is still running today with some 25 members.

Poetry is a literary form that more than any other can be developed and improved by seeking conference with a group of peers. On our active retirement move to Spain, it was our plan to run residential writing weeks at our home in Relleu. We started in 2002. To spread the word to likely local writers I visited the Jávea Book Circle and met an engaging and lively group of compatriots who encouraged me to run some creative writing days. Samantha Muir, the acclaimed classical guitarist, came to one of these gatherings and revealed a great talent for poetry. She suggested we start a poetry workshop and 'Stanza Alacant' was born. Our inaugural meeting was on the 11th of September 2007 at Samantha's home in Pedreguer. There were six around the table. I believe I launched proceedings with a reading of Auden's 'The Fall of Rome'. One of the founder members, Terry Gifford, was visiting lecturer at Alicante University and via a contact there, Teresa Morell-Moll, we were invited to hold our meetings at the University outreach establishment at La Seu, Benissa. They offered us their first class frescoed board room – an ideal venue. It has been the Stanza's meeting place ever since. We have also been able to use the excellent auditorium facility to stage readings from distinguished visiting poets such as Penelope Shuttle, Alfred Corn, Vickie Feaver, Tamar Yoseloff and Judith Barrington. In 2009 we became the first established 'Stanza' of the Poetry Society of Great Britain in Spain. We spawned another Stanza in Mar Menor and there is now a further Stanza in Madrid.

What is a poetry workshop? All the poems in this anthology have been read and been the subject of comment by members of the Stanza at one of our monthly meetings. Many aspirant poets are initially shy of showing their work to a group of strangers but this timidity needs to be overcome if their poetry is to develop. Seeking reaction and comment is a vital part of the creative process. Poetry visits places other literary forms leave alone, it plumbs deeper, explores more and is simply more difficult. Early encouragement and suggestions from peers can prove an essential help in maximizing a poem's potential. In a meeting, discussion ranges all the way from constructive criticism to extravagant praise. Both poles of comment are directed at the page, never the poet. Newcomers to the group soon discover that the poets around the table can be trusted and, by taking note of comments (they are never obliged to agree), it is conspicuous the way their poetic voice improves and becomes more confident.

All those round our table are each in their own way voluntary exiles. For the most part we live in a country that is not our birthplace and as a result we daily experience cultures and ways of life that in many ways remain strange. These perceptions, positive, negative or bewildering are explored in our poetry. Poetry articulates emotions in a way that prose doesn't. It tackles unconscious as well as conscious reactions and thus explores the roots of experience rather than the surface. In this anthology many of the poems react to the feelings of exhilaration that this exciting province of Spain creates and also to experiences that connect with other landscapes – other environments. It is interesting, for example, how in Samantha Muir's 'Montgó and Uluru' she finds the ochre and pinks of local mountains evoking dreamscapes of the rugose and carmine geology of her homeland Australia. Her line 'Red Rock Dreaming' gifted us a title to cover all our explorations and discoveries.

This is the Stanza's first anthology celebrating seven years of enriching activity. If you would like to know more about the meetings and work of the Stanza Alacant Poetry Workshop contact me at christopher @oldolivepress.com.

Christopher North
Chair of Stanza Alacant, Benissa, Alicante.

Contents

Do not leave your poets here
Anne Sefton

(Lakeside sign in the Marina Alta that
should have read: Pets)

Do not leave your poets here.
Their ideas are too uncomfortable.
They make people think
and that should be stopped.
They can't be controlled
or given free rein.

Like some Montessori children they skip around
and sometimes collide
with the romantic novelists
whose characters are playing hard to get
or are hiding in wardrobes.
They do not play the game.
When it comes to hide and seek
they won't be found.
They are elusive to the point of death.

Poets upset the balance of normal thought
with eddies and whirls of dark despair
full of memories of frightened childhoods,
comic careers and broken marriages.

Please don't leave your poets here
when you take the boat on the reservoir

A Castle of Swallows in Spain
Maria Buckingham

The crenellated ruins spy
on huddled homes and
the way marked by ancient scenes
of a passion almost forgotten.

The way to another
faith's fortress
in the lined hills
of a life long gone.

The half burnt tree
in the dry dust
carved by an ancient race
before the now.

What cares the swooping wings
cascading down the air's
steep shafts to lift again,
to create a castle of swallows.

Banu-Issa
Jane Sargeant

A flash of deep blue sky
dry peeling plaster walls, smell of decay
in a white town above a tide-less sea.

Through horseshoe arches an Iberian courtyard.
On red clay tiles *amphorae* clasped in iron
and ceramic pots of bitter orange and clementine.

In the sultry shadows white angel trumpets
hang heavy and still their perfume drifts
calming her *como la adelfa amarga,*

her Dionysian dreams of the Caliph,
his *bufanda* tightly drawn horse-bound
towards her down the narrow street.

Benissa Town
Vivien Johnson

Pedro adjusts his Panama, gnarled knuckles clutch his stick;
eyes dulled by the sun – remembering thirty years ago.
Not just blocks of stone placed one upon another,
columns of basalt forced through the earth's crust.
Then his hands and cement-filled nails laid town bricks,
he shinned up scaffolding, ran along the boards,
ate *bocadillos* from a paper bag –
whistled at the girls below.

Houses huddled as the wind whistled round;
donkeys trampled the narrow streets,
laundry dangled from upstairs windows.
Housewives scrubbed pavements,
puppies tugging at their skirts.

But now it is the turn of others;
children sit on kerb-stones oblivious of passing cars –
soon it will be his son's turn to sit and watch the dancing girls.
Today Miguel plays the trumpet
between benign walls,
a Pied Piper visiting the Stations of the Cross.

Cloud Over Montgó
Anne Sefton

The locals say it is a *mantilla*
for a creaky old lady on her way to Mass.

Or is it a *mantel* - a cosy blanket
used when cold shivers back from stony walls?

The 'Whenwes' say it is a tablecloth
a reminder of Table Mountain.

A tablecloth that shrouds
the rosemary and thyme from sight,

capturing then releasing heady scents
on suffocating nights.

Or is it just a cloud
putting us small humans in the shade?

Benissa
Christopher North

Her town has a street of sorrows
and a street of purity. Bells clong pleasantly
as youths study the torpor of dawdling.
There's a droning old men tertulia on the corner
and nearby, prim wives with a quivering dog.

The Plaza is bathed in honeyed light,
palm shadows, creamy sun-warmed paving
and vanilla scents as doves shuffle their wings.
Her nearby street a corridor of antique stone
where more youths slump beneath a jacaranda.

I want to be alongside as she runs her cake shop -
her neat patisserie of loaves, pastries, buns,
her very centre not falling apart,
her hundreds and thousands, iced architraves,
entablatures and columns – her architecture of cakes,

that drenching doughy odour, sugar dusted,
her busy floury arms, her wrists and elbows.

Montgó and Uluru
Samantha Muir
(Red Rock Dreaming)

Every day you draw me closer
like a pillar of truth I cannot step around.
Red earth, red rock, blue sky – my gambit, and my coda.

You are the face I see
when I pull back the curtain every morning
and you are still there, watching
with your one sad eye,
when I am walking through another life.
Red earth, red rock, blue sky – my mirror, and my blinker.

I see you everywhere I go – on foot, in the car,
amongst the almond groves and the urbanizations,
amongst the pueblos and the fiesta crowds,
always there, leaning out of windows, flaming
above the *Fallas*, walking with the olive pickers,
watching over *Jesús Pobre*.
Always close, just a glance away.
Red earth, red rock, blue sky – my blanket, and my armour.

Above the pine trees and the orange blossom,
beyond the spinifex and the dingo's howl,
morning, noon and dreamtime,
you are there, crooning like a lover.
Red earth, red rock, blue sky – my lullaby, my mantra.

Even at midnight, even in the *gotafria*
when clouds are spilling out of your head
like a mad formula I cannot decipher.
Red earth, red rock, red sky – my gambit and my coda.

Espíritus de Rojo

Rod Davis

Red paints flowers that sway to the Levante
enriches earths that fashion landscapes
fuels music that ignites flamenco
creates lustres that awaken wine

Red unlocks mornings that dance in pools
warms hillsides as goats roam and graze
excites cicadas in the blaze of day
tints fine dust that falls with rain

Red blushes sierras that pierce the sky
romances nightfall in quiet pueblos
pigments shadows in autumn vineyards
ennobles the spirit of Valencian pride

Red grasps hearts that pursue *mantillas*
flames desire within eager youth
inspires images in jasmine dreams
feeds souls that hunger affection

Red incited passion that ripped families apart
shamed blood that drained from so many
unmasked pain that tormented hearts
wrote the poetry of their ache and sorrow

Pepé
Jane Sargeant

Raddled face beneath frayed straw hat
a working life spent on his knees,
fitting a jigsaw of his own making.

Stringy *espadrilles*, a gloved left hand,
sharp iron tool glinting,
in stone-breaking artistry.

Tattered soft broom head
puffs stone dust into the air,
soft rubber blows settle the stones.

Clay water bottle cast down,
meagre ashes scar the soil,
a buckled sardine can.

Pepe stretches out on dusty earth
hands clasped over his body
in wine-dazed ease.

Maserof
Penny Lapenna

In the beginning
a deceptive Eden,
carob-green and aromatic with thyme,
uninhabited, except by fist-sized arachnids
and a lone dog.

In summer verdancy
each sun-split stone springs a bloom
desert-rare and startling -
hot violet, gentian-blue, spike yellow
like flesh in a convent.

The cooling season
still surprises with pregnant heat
and the breath of the *Maserof*
tip-tilts up the valleys runway
to the blue ache of sky.

Standing at full height on a ridge,
child's hand in mine,
I can hear voices rise from the gorge
ethereal, like a dream spoken aloud
the sounds dissipate.

Vista Montgó
Vivien Johnson

The elephant mountain watches the river's mouth,
trunk trailing in Mediterranean water.
He kneels in fields of vines and orange groves.
Pine trees bowing to the wind cling to scarce soil,
cushions of needles settle on rock;
the sun's evening rays rage on the slopes –
new life will blossom there tomorrow.

A patchwork quilt on a mother's birthing bed
a squawking infant and
morning blood with stains of pain,
a child of Aries launched into the world.
Ruled by Mars in anything she'll do,
a firework that flares –
mother will not forsake this cherished child.

As years wheel by
Montgó still kneels
trailing his trunk in the water,
watching for every new birth.

Montgó and Uluru
Samantha Muir

(More Red Rock Dreaming)

¡Vamos! you say. *Let's go.*
To where, I say?
Just climb upon my back.

If only it could be so easy.
But I am like the windmill tower,
sails shorn off,
trying to catch which way the wind blows
and you are the stone I cannot turn.

I circle.
You wait.
I circle.
Stars go in and out
like arrows shooting through an hourglass.

Moon sleeps and wakes,
sleeps and wakes.
Brolga dances,
kookaburra laughs,
rainbow serpent coils around my heart.

I circle.
You wait.
I dream.
You shrug.

Red earth, red rock, red sky
                    - this never-never sunset.

On Mondays in the Mountains
Terry Gifford

On Mondays on the mountain tops
the goats that gave majestic poses
from the crests of passes, the edge of crags,
from afar on Sunday, feast on crumbs
and orange peel, if it's still fresh - now
only their bells disturb the empty breeze.

And on Mondays the swept-horned
wild mountain goats emerge in families
from the trees to traverse screes towards
the highest juniper berries beside the walkers'
trails of tinkling stones - now unseen
in their own element, its silent breeze.

On Mondays along the mountain ridge
the eagle soars on its thermal highway
alert for the scent of death on rocks below,
the boar the hunters injured, limping
along towards it's end, the blind rabbit
riven with disease stinking on the breeze.

And on Mondays in the mountains
wild working beasts are in the breeze.

Rainbow
Jane Sargeant

Montgó purple in rage,
the black sky roars,
rain thrashes the rock.
Across the valley the sun beams.

She steps off the rainbow,
bronze face curved towards the sun,
she seeks a dry terrace to wait
quietly for her moment to shine.

Then the grace of fanned pale skirts
frame a soft deep centre.
Complicated yet undemanding:
Iris innominata.

Arco iris

Jane Sargeant

(Rainbow, translated by José A. González)

Montgó, morada furia,
el cielo negro ruge,
la lluvia fustiga la roca.
En el valle luce un sol resplandeciente.

Se apea del arco iris,
rostro de bronce curvado hacia el sol,
y busca una terraza seca en la que, sosegada,
pueda esperar la hora de encenderse.

Entonces, el gracioso abanico de sus pálidas faldas
enmarca un centro blando, profundo.
Complicada mas poco exigente:
Iris innominata.

Lluvia adentro
José A. González

Introduzco las manos en la lluvia
como un furtivo,
sin luz,
sin ayuda de arco iris;
solo las manos desnudas
en el núcleo del agua.

Into the rain

José A. González

(Translated)

I introduce my hands into the rain
like a poacher,
with no light,
unaided by a rainbow;
only my bare hands
into the core of water.

The Goatherd
Vivien Johnson

The Sirocco charges down the valley –
a demented dragon's breath,
dried earth scorched yet again;
goats and sheep munch desiccated rosemary and thyme.

Pedro huddles in the cave; battered hat pulled down,
threadbare clothes give little comfort.
He shares his home with geckos and snakes.
His dog will warn him if foxes attack his stock.

Perhaps Consuelo will come with food?

The wind scrapes the mountains,
Sahara sand covers glacial rocks –
forked lightning rips the sky
lighting up sierra needle-crags.

The rain comes shyly – apologetic –
disturbing the sun-baked world.
Then torrents lash down – rage –
transparent whips slash from the sky.
Thunder crashes like the sound of battle.

Pedro knew the storm would come.
He had felt the changes –
had watched clouds like quilts
rolling over the mountains' lips.

Afterwards new shoots force their way to the light;
crystal waters bubble from inhospitable rock.
A mountain pine clings to a soilless ridge –
sheep no longer pant in the midday sun.
Goats' bells jingle-jangle on still air.

Sierra Bernia
Jill Lanchbery

The blank canvas beckons,
urging me to fill the starkness
with dancing images that will
transform the emptiness and
bring it meaning.

I fail to concentrate,
scratch my ear, and then
glance from the window and see
the sprawling mass of Sierra Bernia.
And the inspiration that has eluded
is laid out in front of me,
her feminine curves bathed in
orange streaks of light.

I struggle to give it life,
to find words that will express my thoughts
and fill the page with colour.
Of brightly painted *fincas*
straggling across her slopes,
punctuated by dots of yellow gorse
and pink valerian.

Terracotta tiles glow in the golden light
and dark eagles scissor the sky,
cutting through the clouds
to emerge clear and new
into blue certainty.

And suddenly it is enough.

Joaquina, Parcent
Jacqueline Cotterill

Slanting sun creeps under washhouse eaves,
casts twigged shadow on water scoured stone,
warms ridged spine and cotton wisp hair.

Joaquina washes, sparrow framed,
paper skin, plum stained, vein traced hands
pummel wool in nature's numbing softener.

Back hunched, rheumy gaze steadfast,
rhythmic plunging, scrubbing, wringing,
mind wandering, memories flooding as water flows.

Face furrowed like river carved rock,
hooded eyes blink into sunlight.
Hauls to arthritic hip her waterlogged load.

Painstakingly, step by dogged step,
eighty years of resistance meanders
the cobbled climb home.

Blankets dance on rooftop terrace
as sun flushed breeze billows,
swathes Joaquina's restful sleep.

Silver Filigree
John David Moorhouse

It was such a lovely jewel box.
I could not resist it and bought it on the spot.
At home I examined it more closely.
The inside was lined with a silver filigree skin.

I touched the skin and that was when it trapped me.
Before I knew it the skin had wrapped itself round my hand
pulling at my wrist, growing up my arm,
spreading over my body like a silver net.

Now you are mine, said the woman in blue.
Where had she come from? She seemed familiar.
She seemed to know my thoughts.
I could feel her controlling me.

Everything was covered by silver filigree,
from the trees in the garden to the distant sierra.
The light was blinding as my eyelids closed,
forced shut by the weight of silver filigree.

The Bull of the Bernia
Terry Gifford

I think it was my curiosity that caused it
and perhaps you were right that it had
put us both in danger high on the open
mountainside amongst the Bernia's bulls
where a simple afternoon of walking the track,
grazing bulls below us, suddenly turned violent.
Was it because I stopped? Was it because I wondered
what that young bull saw behind my eyes
from its still, staring, glassy eyes locked on mine
that it answered my question with an explosion
of legs, muscle, horns that carried a hurt of the heart
into my outstretched walking poles in its head?

Into my outstretched walking poles in its head,
legs, muscles, horns that carried a hurt of the heart,
that answered my question with an explosion
from its still, staring, glassy eyes locked on mine
was what that young bull saw behind my eyes.
Was it because I stopped? Was it because I wondered
grazing bulls below us suddenly turned violent
where a simple afternoon of walking the track
on the mountainside amongst the Bernia's bulls
put us both in danger, high and open?
And perhaps you were right that it had.
I think it was my curiosity that caused it.

El Toro del Bernia

(Tanslated by José A. González)

Creo que fue mi curiosidad la que lo provocó
y quizá tuvieras razón al decir que así había sido
que nos había puesto a ambos en peligro en la elevada y franca
ladera en medio de los toros del Bernia
allá donde una simple tarde de caminata por el sendero,
con unos toros que pastaban abajo, de pronto se volvió violenta.
¿Fue porque me detuve? ¿Fue porque me pregunté
qué había visto aquel novillo en el fondo de mis ojos
con sus ojos inmóviles, desorbitados, vidriosos, fijos en mí
por lo que aquel contestó mi pregunta con un estallido
de patas, músculo, cuernos que llevaron un dolor del corazón
hasta mis bastones extendidos dentro de su cabeza?

Hasta mis bastones extendidos dentro de su cabeza,
patas, músculo, cuernos que llevaron un dolor del corazón,
que contestó mi pregunta con un estallido
con sus ojos inmóviles, desorbitados, vidriosos, fijos en mí
había visto aquel novillo en el fondo de mis ojos.
¿Fue porque me detuve? ¿Fue porque me pregunté
por lo que unos toros que pastaban abajo de pronto
                                    se volvieron violentos
allá donde una simple tarde de caminata por el sendero
de la ladera en medio de los toros del Bernia
nos había puesto a ambos en peligro, elevado y franco?
Y quizá tuvieras razón al decir que así había sido.
Creo que fue mi curiosidad la que lo provocó.

Donkey
Terry Gifford

What Valencian counting rhymes
were chanted between the narrow walls
of Pas de Comptador, allowing one goat
at a time and always a funnelled wind?

Today we could breach it in our 4x4,
the sun already set behind Cabeçó d'Or
and on the old road name, Camí Real.
We looked down the length of the Val d'Arc

towards home, a return to the womb, rich
with shadows among olives and almond trees,
and the white veins of tracks and trails
we knew so well from years of walking here.

But we did not know a single donkey
left in the Val d'Arc and here was one
standing still and ghostly pale at the foot
of the steep rutted slope from the pass.

Its long trailing rope told the story.
It was reluctant to get quite so close
to the tree to which we tied it,
using all the rope in a donkey-proof knot.

Questions, questions, as we drove on down
the long valley floor until we saw a man:
leather jacket, scarred brown face, wild hair.
Did he know anyone who kept a donkey?

That donkey, he said without a smile, *eats
and eats all day getting fatter and fatter.
So each evening I take her for a walk.
I was wondering where she was.*

Well, we tied her to a tree back there.
We thought she had escaped. Sorry.
He was gracious, this hermit from
the highest house in the valley.

Thank you, he said, turning back.
What Valencian curses carried on the wind
that night? And in the talk at the next market,
how many donkeys were in this story?

Festera
Jacqueline Cotterill

She slept, head placed
precisely on sofa arm,
gown laid waiting. I am
transfixed by her loveliness.

Dancing till sunrise, tired legs
dragged to the salon's chair,
hair rolled and twirled,
adorned with silk flowers.

I wake her gently,
revived with black coffee,
she shakes off sleep,
slips on white satin, transforms.

Pearl drops gleam through
black lace cobwebs cascading
from her crowning comb,
mantilla majestic on proud head.

Silver shoes, gold threaded sash,
fan fluttering, flickering like
humming birds wings in midday heat.
Drums beat, the band nears.

She takes her place, framed by
kissing palms, waiting for
her suited *Festero* to offer his
arm whilst the brass serenades.

All Souls' Day 2010, Sella
Terry Gifford

A chill wind swept
the souls of the departed
through the best-dressed cemetery,
the frailty of flowers
under the bright mountain
bringing tears to the eyes
of the living, best-dressed,
wandering there, lost
in their vivid memories,
their stories soon to be lost
on the unrelenting winds of time.

But today they live,
these stories, small snatches
of whole lives: 'His last words were,
Look after each other.'
'She lived until ninety-seven
and still had all her marbles.'
'This photo is of his second
wife – a good mother to his kids.'
And so many questions
that cannot now be answered.
The gravedigger walks with a stick.

Aceite
Christopher North

The Mediterranean is not a sea of salt
but a sea of oil:
golden green – a fall of it
at the pillars of Hercules,
a golden mist in the air
that drizzles over mountains,
praderas, solanas, carrasquetas,
Umbrian hills, the long bone of Crete,
flower-filled groves of Cyprus,
Minoan, Ischian, Ionian, Tyrrhenian islands,
the Cyclades, the Dodecanese,
ancient cones of Etna and Stromboli.
The swish and wash of silver leaves,
a flurry before the gold, the leaves of stars
and wood of twisting, writhing limbs.

Olive's peace of lazy luncheons,
of slow food, drenched with Arbequina,
Picual or Cornicabra – the oils of Kalamata,
or from the ancient Venetian groves of Corfu.

Oil to glisten flesh, to lighten shadow
from a golden apple of the sun,
to gleaming cherry-stone of moon;
bottled flood – deep root, tap root
of the Mediterranean.

The drone of conversation beneath olive boughs,
as a swallow dips through the clipped branches,
wind moving the green olives,
from green to purple to black,
the wind taking their blush to shine.

Aceite
Christopher North
(Tanslated by José A. González)

No es el Mediterráneo un mar de sal
sino de aceite:
caudal de verde dorado
vertido en las columnas de Hércules,
neblina de oro en el aire
que salpica los montes,
las praderas, las solanas, las carrascas,
los cerros de Umbría, el hueso largo de Creta,
los floridos olivares de Chipre,
Isquia, las islas Minoicas, Jónicas y Tirrénicas,
las Cícladas, el Dodecaneso,
los conos antiguos del Etna y del Estrómboli.
El vaivén y el rumor de las hojas de plata,
ráfaga antecesora del oro, hojas de las estrellas
y madera de miembros torcidos, contorsionados.

Pacífico aceite de almuerzos perezosos,
de lentos guisos, regados con arbequina,
picual o cornicabra, o aceites de Kalamata
o de añejos olivares venecianos de Corfú.

Aceite que lustra la carne, que aligera la sombra
de dorada manzana de sol
a luciente pepita de luna;
marea embotellada, honda raíz, raíz
primaria del Mediterráneo.

Murmullo de conversación bajo ramas de olivo,
ramas pinzadas que cruza una golondrina,
mientras el viento guía las olivas verdes
del verde hacia el morado, del morado hacia el negro,
y convierte su pátina en esplendor.

Gathering Almonds
Christopher North

Bamboo taps happy almonds to our net.
They are anxious to fall and fill our world.

Scrabbling fingers shuck husks all day
until the dusky gathering to night,

when what we eat, read and dream of
are their falling helmets,

the scuttle of earwigs, scabbed finger ends -
all in orbits of almonds and the almond trees.

Almonds encrust door-jambs and handles.
The living room becomes an almond grove.

Words from your mouth are almonds falling
and more tumble from your anxious hands

as the floor becomes a crunchy husk track.
The telephone brings news of almonds.

Shelled almonds a carpet in the sun
as fingers gather from one last sapling

and arms ache from the laden sacks.
And the almonds are always silent

but would sing of their beginnings
in a frill of mawkish blossom,

the fumbling bees, swelling through heat,
their glad tumble to our blessed nets,

and the stripping away of veils, shellac and skins
to a final, brief, pure white nakedness.

In my Spanish Village
Maria Buckingham

It has died, that regal palm,
which graced Maria's garden
for ninety years,
before I came next door.

The crown has gone
the browning fronds just hang.
She stares and
whispers *¡Triste!*

In José's garden
an old stately friend
is trimmed to a tall stump.
I shake my head, *Weevils?*

Es natural José shrugs.
The oranges were good this season.
Bags appeared hanging
from the front door knob.

José's little dog
chases the oranges
as we walk through the groves
and along the lanes

our four dogs in excited tow.
A heavy scent hangs in the air
where the bees drum
and a nightingale out-bids its rivals.

¡Buenos dias! it is market day,
Maria leaves, and I sit
on the swing seat, dreaming
as my cat sleeps.

Un mundo de ocío
José A. González

Poder pisar el suelo
descalzo,
ahora que es primavera.

Ojos cerrados:
se filtra entre los trinos
la luz de abril.

Gato dormido,
cada vez pesa menos
en mi regazo.

La telaraña
que hay en la regadera
atrapa flores.

La mariposa
sigue a los caminantes:
llevan luz en los hombros.

Plumón de nubes
meciéndose en el fondo
de la piscina.

Cuando atardece
el eco del murciélago relumbra
detrás del limonero.

No hay ni una estrella;
solo los grillos llenan
el cielo.

Duda la luz,
las toallas no se secan:
llegó el otoño.

A World of Dew
José A. González
(Translated)

Being able to step on the floor
barefoot,
now that spring has come.

Eyes closed –
April light percolating
through birdsong.

Sleeping cat,
becoming increasingly weightless
on my lap.

The cobweb
inside the watering can
traps flowers.

A butterfly
follows the hikers –
they wear light on their shoulders.

Cloud down
swaying in the bottom
of the swimming pool.

In the evening
the echo of the bat glitters
behind the lemon tree.

There is no single star –
only the crickets fill
the sky.

Light hesitates,
towels don't dry –
autumn has come.

Playa de las Marinas
José A. González

La obra del viento
es agitarlo todo
y quedarse prendido en su luz.

Cuando sopla en la playa, esta levita
unos instantes,
y nosotros con ella.

Luego, brillamos.

Las Marinas Beach

José A. González

(Translated)

The wind's work
is to shake all things
and linger in their light.

As it blows the beach levitates
for a few seconds,
and we levitate too.

Then, we shine.

Sunday Morning at the Arenal
Jill Lanchbery

The infant stretches cat-like in the buggy,
sun kissing her new pink limbs
as she basks in the warmth.
Her lullaby the sea, the whisper of the waves as they
whoosh across the pebbles,
the hum of bees exploring a crimson oleander.

The boy rocks on his chair,
scuffed Reeboks kicking a tattoo on the table leg,
as bubbles of treacly coca-cola pop
from the end of the red striped straw.
One eye focuses on a chocolate sprinkled ice-cream,
the other on the flat screen of his Game Boy.

The girl adjusts her replica Raybans,
plugs the shell of her ear with the plastic dome of the iPod,
and as a gaggle of boys comes into view,
fine-tunes her pose,
pretends not to see them,
honey coloured legs swaying nonchalantly to the beat.

The man takes a deep slug of San Miguel, sighs contentedly,
rubs the embryonic mound that rises below his ribs,
pushes out his chest to display the Barça logo,
then remembers,
fiddles with his Smart Phone, shrugs and decides that maybe
tomorrow is soon enough and once more raises the bottle to his lips.

The woman studies each in turn,
longs to grasp the moment,
to clutch it tightly in the clenched ball of her hand.
Instead she orders them,
Smile, say cheese!
Squeezes the button and records the scene.

Golden Shoes
John Catanach

When skirts were short and hair was long
and Biba ruled the fashion trade
when Mary Quant had conquered Vogue
then it was that we were made

With delicate sole and spiky heel
long straps like drovers' whips
a happening in soft gilded hide
then London swung, like Monroe's hips

The Beatles sang and Hendrix played
Mick Jagger in his fancy gear
in London's clubs each night we twirled
we lived and loved each long, long year

But now we're scuffed and bruised and torn
heels cracked and beauty passed
we look back across our long, long life
all the way from last to last

On a tip in this dusty road
our soles depart, we're very old
on a bed of marmalade jars
just Silver Shred among the gold.

A Walk in the Past
Vivien Johnson

Gentle folds and rugged crags
where trees cling to escarpments;
and paths of yellow like a child's sandpit
lead to Benidorm to Mediterranean-merge.
One red roof strident in the landscape,
an open wound against the terracotta,
shuttered windows and silent streets.

I see El Cid riding tortuous tracks,
his troops Spanish stallions mounted;
armour and weapons creak and clank.
Battle-streets run river-red;
fight's acrid smell on men's
shirts and tattered breeches.
Hunger – unassuaged.

Huddled villagers behind closed doors;
children hide in mothers' skirts –
frightened animals.
The soldiers' horses snorting smoke –
the sound of forged iron
clatters on cobbled stones.

My vision has fled.

Now, *Melónes*, a farmer cries;
sells only a few from the back of his van.
It's fiesta, the village sleeps.
Later the people will ogle and exclaim
over fireworks from the square.

I scale the mountains to follow El Cid,
my footprints held in silent sand.
A red roof slashes the barren landscape.

Family Gathering 16th January 2013
Anne Sefton

An ordinary morning, we walked the dogs
Ben with him, Toots and Freddy with me.

We met on the path through Jabali
wood, halfway round as we usually do.

In our gravelled garden I searched
for flowers for my father's breakfast tray

I found jasmine and a creamy white rose,
an *Iceberg*. A bee hovered over the late

morning glory and I remembered my mother
saying bees brought you luck or money.

In the house the phone rang and
from a thousand miles away

we heard the mewling cries of newly
born twins seeking out my daughter's breast.

When There Isn't Time
Penny Lapenna

You marshall thoughts like dominos, careful
to avoid one last tap. The page erupts in its blaring white
signal of the endless now. Knowing that

you should really set out to collect them from the school gates
or there will be tears. Put down the cup, the mouse, the pen
and drag on the non-slip boots, all too mundane for poetry

but woven into your day since the redundancy tossed
you back into the maelstrom of your four-square life.
It bites, that ankle-nip you tense for but can't avoid.

How can there not be time, as if poems grow
like nine-month conceptions, after the futon excitement,
after the furore becomes the roar of daily traffic?

I'm late. I've missed them. They have already set out
for the birthday party in the café on Calle Dalt, up the hill
through the square of Renaults and Berlingos.

Bald bellies over combats disturb me in the plaza
the careless presence of a child only a skin's wall away
from harm. There is no time, this time, to tell them.

Find them among fifteen excitable heads. I am removed from the room
floating with the smoke skeins, mere inches above
each separate insistent forehead. The world turns

on a pin; a dream of longing packed into a sci-fi movie
in that square inch in my periphery, above the coffee-cup rattle
and her face where time has passed while no-one noticed.

To make a difference. To be remembered. To be eternal
in the blush of youth, an echoing chain gang of family passes
through generations in the shape of a tea-stained birthmark.

The baby hiccoughs. She leans its head on her arm
like there is all the time in the world to worry about him,
but not now, when her own pulse races, and skips.

I take their bags. Coats. There will be time to write
after they have learned trigonometry, epidermal layers,
and the intricacies of conveying their hearts desires

to me, as though I could fulfill them. If only. The cats
yawn, removing themselves from their feline Ouroboros
to make space at the PC. I must read more Vonnegut.

Remember Me to Montgó
Rod Davis

i.m. María Luisa

I gaze across our Montgó valley
to misty far Sierras,
watch the early blush of morning
expose their virgin beauty
that day will later hide in
erotic blues and purples.
Almond groves and fields emerge
as rising sun wets softer hills,
an echo of her waking body
that used to herald dawn.

Smoke rises from a lazy fire,
a stroke from an artist's pallet
unmoving on the canvas sky,
only to vanish in an instant
to become another memory.
An image of Jávea bay unfolds,
shimmering in a frame
of aromatic pine and eucalyptus,
a hint of her intimate perfume
that fired our time of love.

Rasping crickets and cicadas,
noiseless now in Montgó forests.
Bees no longer hum their flight
through jasmin-laden air.
A dry rose falls silently
in the dusky evening shadows,
while hibiscus fold their petals
to cocoon their daytime boldness
as a homage to her allure
that filled so many nights.

Grapefruit ripen on a tree,
pomegranates lie red with jewels,
olives blacken getting fatter.
Mangoes offer subtle flavour
and oranges promise with their juice
a celebration of abundant life,
while thyme and rosemary beg
pick me, squeeze me, taste my spice.
I mourn my fragile woman
who rewarded every day.

Recuerdos
Jill Lanchbery

Once each yellow stone and
grey streaked rock
represented a gift of time and love,
when he carried her across
the sandstone threshold of their first home,
the roofless shell open to the elements,
and paused, stroking the rain from her hair
and licking the residue of their
shared Rioja from her mouth.

Once she sat with their child
his soft limbs warmed by the summer sun,
limpet lips sucking life from the golden
aureole of her breast,
stroking the feathery down of his head
and wanting nothing more
than the yellow stone and
grey streaked rock,
cradled in avenues of orange groves.

Once there were only oranges
and grapes and time to sit in the sun.
When he was content to tend the crops,
his son by his side,
their brown bodies steeped in sunshine
and citrus and muscatel,
and they would stroll nonchalantly
behind the horse drawn plough
taking pride in the neat red furrows.

It was the orange groves that were first to go.
The *extranjeros* came with their promises
and bulging wallets and bulldozers,
and churned up the rich red earth,
discarding bright orange fruit,
tearing down the yellow stone,
and grey streaked rock,
replacing it with their concrete god.

Now they stand on the balcony of their fifth floor flat
remembering what used to be.
Seeing only where there were oranges and grapes,
abandoned shells of promised dreams.
Spilled tins of yellow paint, crumbling grey blocks,
ghostly skeletons of houses.
He smelling of dust and she of despair.
Their son's dreams crushed.

Ghost of Fascism
Jacqueline Cotterill

Demonstration at Parcent Council's decision to
approve the building of 1500 houses on the mountain

Village at war, outrage flaming,
shouts echo from thronged streets,
calling, calling, I flood in.

I move among them, inhale their rage,
feel resistance as protest swirls
round the rain-lashed crowd.

Armoured with anger, beyond
my reach, their fire of justice
melts my hoary breath.

I blanket the valley, cloak
the mountain, smother slopes
threatened by insatiable greed.

I seep into the village, scarves held
to faces to keep out my chill, creep
under doors bringing icy unease.

Haunted still by Franco's ghosts,
exposed by bitter memories,
I slip stealthily into their souls.

Here hides confusion, webs of guilt,
loyalties torn, I scratch thin skin
and blood of fear freely flows.

Whisper, don't speak, stay indoors,
stay away. Let others fight, remember,
what if, what if, what if.

Probe deep and reach black seam of
pain. Whose side were you on,
who did what, who once killed who?

Old divisions revived, Franco lives,
banners torn down, backs coldly
turned, muffled talk in silent streets.

Ancient enmity stifles debate,
I devour their derision, feed on
their fury, taste venal desires.

Feel the light fighting back, sun
torching holes in my ghostly wrap
as the untouched voices raise.

Howl one last haunt, leave souls
corrupted for lucre's false gain.
Battle lines drawn in Spanish soil.

El Toque de Silencio
John Catanach

*Spanish Civil War extracts adapted from
recollections of the 40 living UK members of the
International Brigades, 'The Last of the Brigade',
The Guardian, 10/11/2000.*

*Hotel comments based on recent postings on
Trip Advisor*

▶Teruel 1937, the worst winter for 20 years.
The prison camp, had no windows, just bars,
no bedding, no heating, we slept on the stone floor.
No sanitation, fleas and rats everywhere, filthy,
plagued with lice, we were starving,
a small loaf each day kept us alive.
We tried to stay cheerful despite conditions
and the guards brutality, some died.
We made chess sets from bits of bread
and waited for the Spring to come.

▷*Staff at the Teruel Parador are inattentive.
We'd had better breakfast at other Paradores,
lukewarm eggs, ham…only plain yoghurts.
Teruel offers lots of street life,
good restaurants and lively bars,
there are many ancient buildings.
In 1937 a decisive battle
had been fought here we were told,
many casualties on both sides apparently
but we couldn't find a memorial anywhere.*

▶I was at Belchite in August '37
tending the wounded in the church.
One young Spaniard was in a terrible way
burned all over, his clothes gone.
I didn't see him as my enemy,
just a young man in awful trouble.
This was the first time I'd seen a casualty
so burned and in total torment.
A stretcher-bearer used a nearby rifle
and ended his agony with a single shot.

▷I'll be arriving at Belchite from Zaragosa
is there dedicated parking for visiting the ruins?
I understand it was possible to wander around
this wrecked town for free, now it costs 6 euros
per person for a guided tour...disgraceful!
Postscript:The weather was bad
so we decided against the long tour
and took a quick wander down town.
It's possible to see quite a lot that way,
including the local wrecked church.

▶I was the first correspondent into Guernica.
Soldiers stood sobbing like children,
the smell of burning flesh was nauseating,
houses collapsed into the inferno.
About a hundred refugees were screaming
as a wall of fire surrounded and engulfed them.
I'm still haunted by the sight, the cruel nightmare,
the charred bodies of innocent women and children
huddled together in death in the cellar of a house
designated a refugio...a place of safety.

▷Our room at Hotel Guernika was clean
and comfortable for a provincial hotel.
It's just a short walk down-town
and close to several museums,
Guernica is full of good restaurants.
However complimentary toiletries are inadequate,
our shower curtains leaked,
our room had no fridge and a very small TV,
Wi-Fi was available though very slow.
Pleasant staff but speak little English.

Opposites Attract
Anne Sefton

Cool is a marble shelf in a north-facing pantry
home-paddled yellow butter resting on a plate.

Hot is a south-facing bedroom in a Spanish July,
damp sheets rumpled at the foot of the bed.

There: asparagus beds, rhubarb and roses.
Here: olive oil, peaches and pomegranates.

From green fields and waterside gardens
to parched soil guardian spiky succulents.

In between an average life of working,
home and waiting for this Other. Here.

Sierra del Carrascal de Parcent
Jacqueline Cotterill

Eyes open she lies before me.
As lustrous moonlight bathes her slopes,
the shimmering pearl slips over the sierra.
Darkness reigns, till soft red creeps.
Breaking dawn fires her craggy flanks,
etching sharp shadows, greys wake to green.
In drowsy gaze, flocks wing swooping
from rocks to rooftops, mountain of moods
heralds the coming day.

Womanly to her granite core,
clothed by climate's vagaries,
El Carrascal's spirit mirrors my own.
Today we're bright, spring like,
sunlight warming, not yet beating down
with summer's blistering haze.
On sombre days we share suffering;
bluffs draped in misty mourning,
breath laboured, dampness invades.

Glooming mists blown away, sculptured
reliefs exposed then veiled as billowing clouds
tumble down like custard over pudding.
El Carrascal stands proud, shadows spaghetti of
tangled streets, pine clad vista in windows framed,
imposing, unmoving, untamed.
Strength of ages, unspoken witness,
terraced by Moors, refuge from war,
fountains of life spring from underground veins.

Serene Sierra threatened by avarice,
slashing scars of slick cement, trees razed,
hills pockmarked in contagious white rash.
Where fires raged, houses raise, mushroom sprawl
fuelled by flagrant greed, fanned by ignorance,
the migrant's dream kindling destruction.
Eyes open, she lies before me.
Blood red sky foretells my loss.
I rise to fight; while souls inflame, hope remains.

Barranc Anochecida
Christopher North

Above the sugar froth of almond blossom
the Panaderia gable and flank of Pepé's bar,
the church tower shadow fingers slipping tiles.
The Street of Miracles climbs to a ragged Calvario
a vague zig zag up to the chapel plaza.

From this circle of chipped disciples a path ascends
to the ruined teeth and sockets of the Moor's castle.
Behind, the sierra's thigh moves to purple
and above the top pines, the higher Aitana ridge,
a prickle of aerials and communication domes.

Over them the gathering gleam of a gibbous moon,
Venus to its side a torch and, still hidden,
a dust mote stream of galactic light and beyond that
billions upon billions of swarming galaxies
each with villages, wines, sounds of water running,

fragrances, books left face down on boundary walls
and evening crickets whirring a single rhythmic note.

Contributors

Maria Buckingham
When I retired from working in the computing industry and photography, I developed many interests including writing poetry, music, art and crafts. The move to Spain in 2005 enabled me to join the Stanza Alacant and to develop techniques. These are my first published poems but I have had short stories and scientific papers published.

John Catanach
John spent 50 years in advertising, at one time handling the publicity for Ronnie Scott's Jazz Club in Soho where he never paid to go in. Current ambition is to play the trumpet like Buck Clayton. He is married to Gill and they flit regularly between Jávea and Bournemouth.

Jacqueline Cotterill
Jacqueline Cotterill has lived in Spain for 24 years and is the Deputy Mayor of her small village. She is a campaigner for environmental protection and property and voting rights for European residents in Spain. She has written articles about Spanish life and politics, short stories and a collection of poetry.

Rod Davis
Rod ran a design business for 25 years in London before dropping it all to work for charity. He took over a family property in Jávea in 1986 where he now lives and since retiring Rod has returned to painting, his first love. Writing has always been part of his life and he sees poetry as an extension of his art.

Terry Gifford

Terry lives in the village of Sella for part of the year and is the author of seven collections of poetry, most recently, with Christopher North, *The Other Side of Aguilar* (Oversteps Books, 2011), a dual language book in English and Spanish. *Green Voices: Understanding Contemporary Nature Poetry* (Manchester University Press, 1995; second edition 2011) was acclaimed as 'the first comprehensive British study of contemporary ecopoetry'. He is the author/editor of four books on Ted Hughes and also author of *Reconnecting With John Muir: Essays in Post-Pastoral Practice* (2006) and *Pastoral* (1999), Terry Gifford is Senior Research Fellow and Profesor Honorifico at the University of Alicante, Spain and Visiting Professor at the Centre for Writing and Environment, Bath Spa University, UK.

José A. González

Born in Spain. He is a translator and a poet. He has lived in Italy, Switzerland and the USA. He lives currently in Denia (Spain). He has published, in collaboration with Juan C. Valdovinos, a haiku poetry cum photography book, *Haikugraphies* (Shinden, Barcelona, 2011, four language version: Spanish, English, Catalan and Japanese).

Vivien Johnson

I have lived in the Jalon Valley, Spain, for thirteen years. I have been lucky enough to have had prose and poetry published here and in U.K. I have won the Segora 2013 International Poetry Competition, and have been a runner up several times in other competitions. I have also broadcast my work, prose and poetry, on two U.K. radio stations.

Jill Lanchbery

Jill grew up in Zambia and now lives in Lliber, on Spain's Costa Blanca. She has had articles and short stories published and been placed in several international short story competitions as well as writing two contemporary novels, *A Bucket of Ashes* and *Griefs and Fears*. These are her first published poems.

Penny Lapenna

Penny was born in London, and worked as a T-shirt designer, landscape gardener, youth arts worker, education consultant and publishing assistant, before moving to Spain in 2001. Her experience of bringing up three children in a tiny mountain village left little time for poetry, which is exactly why she had to write it.

John David Moorhouse

David lives in Baladrar/Benissa; retired 15 years, 78 years young; loves the discipline and freedom of poetry; has written more than 100 poems and many short stories; still heading to 'new places'.

Samantha Muir

Sam is a professional classical guitarist and occasional ukulele player. Her other interests include writing poetry and walking in the mountains. In 2009 she collaborated with photographer Josie Elias to produce a book of poetry and photographs of the Marina Alta entitled, *The Alchemy of Thyme and Rubble*. In 2012 Sam won 2nd prize in the Sherborne Literary Festival Poetry Competition.

Christopher North

I have written poetry all my life but with serious focus from 1989 when I joined a workshop with John Fairfax, founder of the Arvon Foundation. My first major success was a third place in the National Poetry Competition in 1995. My first pamphlet collection *A Mesh of Wires* was short listed for the Forward Prize for 'Best First Collection' in 1999. I won the Poetry on the Lake's 'Silver Wyvern' prize in 2007, published my first full collection *Explaining the Circumstances* in 2010, my joint bi-lingual collection with fellow Stanza member Terry Gifford in 2011 and will be publishing my second full collection *The Night Surveyor* in 2014. Since 2002 I have facilitated Residential poetry study weeks at the Almassera Vella in Relleu, Alicante. www.oldolivepress.com.

Jane Sargeant

Jane Sargeant lives in Jávea. For twenty years she has enjoyed exploring the history, literature, art and landscape of Spain. A regular visitor to the King's Lynn Fiction and Poetry festivals.

Anne Sefton-Parlevliet

Anne was born to a saint from St Helena and a Dutch father in Oxford, has lived in Italy, London and Sussex. Favourite job teaching TEFL. She moved to Jávea in 1985 with an infant daughter. Writes short stories and poems and is fascinated with the meaning of words.

Lightning Source UK Ltd.
Milton Keynes UK
UKOW03n1444220614

233854UK00002B/2/P